DUKE ELLINGTON

Legendary Composer and Bandleader

Celebrating **BLACK ARTISTS**

DUKE ELLINGTON

Legendary Composer and Bandleader

Enslow Publishing
101 W. 23rd Street
Suite 240
New York, NY 10011
USA
enslow.com

**CHARLOTTE ETINDE-CROMPTON AND
SAMUEL WILLARD CROMPTON**

Published in 2020 by Enslow Publishing, LLC.
101 W. 23rd Street, Suite 240, New York, NY 10011

Copyright © 2020 by Enslow Publishing, LLC.

All rights reserved.

No part of this book may be reproduced by any means without the written permission of the publisher.

Library of Congress Cataloging-in-Publication Data

Names: Crompton, Samuel Willard, author. | Etinde-Crompton, Charlotte, author.
Title: Duke Ellington : legendary composer and bandleader / Samuel Willard Crompton and Charlotte Etinde-Crompton.
Description: New York : Enslow Publishing, 2020 | Series: Celebrating black artists | Audience: Grade 5–8. | Includes bibliographical references and index.
Identifiers: LCCN 2018058551| ISBN 9781978503564 (library bound) | ISBN 9781978505315 (pbk.)
Subjects: LCSH: Ellington, Duke, 1899–1974—Juvenile literature. | African American jazz musicians—Biography—Juvenile literature. | Jazz musicians—United States—Biography—Juvenile literature.
Classification: LCC ML3930.E44 C76 2019 | DDC 781.65092 [B] —dc23
LC record available at https://lccn.loc.gov/2018058551

Printed in China

To Our Readers: We have done our best to make sure all website addresses in this book were active and appropriate when we went to press. However, the author and the publisher have no control over and assume no liability for the material available on those websites or on any websites they may link to. Any comments or suggestions can be sent by email to customerservice@enslow.com.

Photo Credits: Cover, pp. 3, 50–51, 55, 61, 86 Michael Ochs Archives/Getty Images; pp. 8–9 Ben Martin/Archive Photos/Getty Images; p. 11 Paul Hoeffler/Redferns/Getty Images; pp. 16–17 Print Collector/Hulton Archive/Getty Images; p. 21 The Washington Post/Getty Images; pp. 24, 41, 46–47 Bettmann/Getty Images; pp. 26–27 Underwood Archives/Archive Photos/Getty Images; pp. 32–33 Science History Images/Alamy Stock Photo; pp. 36–37, 68–69 JP Jazz Archive/Redferns/Getty Images; p. 43 GAB Archive/Redferns/Getty Images; p. 52 Metronome/Archive Photos/Getty Images; pp. 58–59 Keystone-France/Gamma-Keystone/Getty Images; pp. 64–65 Earl Theisen Collection/Archive Photos/Getty Images; p. 73 Evans/Hulton Archive/Getty Images; pp. 74–75 Robert Parent/The LIFE Images Collection/Getty Images; p. 78 Afro Newspaper/Gado/Archive Photos/Getty Images; pp. 80–81 Everett Collection Historical/Alamy Stock Photo; p. 83 Bill Wagg/Redferns/Getty Images; pp. 88–89 Central Press/Hulton Archive/Getty Images; pp. 90–91 John Pratt/Hulton Archive/Getty Images.

Contents

1 Rebirth at Fifty-Seven 7

2 A Capital Time 15

3 A Medley of Music 23

4 Leader of the Band 31

5 Sudden Fame 40

6 That Swing 48

7 Top of the World 58

8 Adversity 68

9 Return to the Top 77

10 Ellington in Perspective 85

   Chronology 93

   Chapter Notes 97

   Glossary 99

   Further Reading 100

   Index 101

   About the Authors 104

Chapter 1

Rebirth at Fifty-Seven

In July 1956, Duke Ellington and his world-famous orchestra were on their last legs. They knew it. The music critics knew it. The fans, who had previously embraced Ellington and his particular form of musical magic, had come to know it, too.

The Duke did not swing the way he had in earlier days. His musicians were quarrelsome, with some being occasionally jailed for the possession of heroin. But it was not all the fault of the Duke or his musicians. Time had passed them by.

The handsome, urbane, and forever classy Duke Ellington first led his band to fame in the 1930s, the decade that came to be known as the Big Band era. Americans from all walks of life flocked to concert and dance halls to hear Ellington and his band, as well as Benny Goodman and dozens of other big bands.

At times, it seemed as if the Big Band Era would never end—as if Ellington, Goodman, and the others would make money and light up cityscapes for the rest of their lives. But American music took a sharp turn in the years immediately following the Second World War. Young people now flocked to hear solo entertainers, such as Frank Sinatra, who was an admirer of Ellington. The big bands drew smaller audiences each year.

To be sure, there was a hardcore group of fans that did not go away. Some listeners vowed they would stick with Duke Ellington forever. But by the spring of 1956, Ellington was reduced to providing music at an ice rink in Brooklyn, New York. His best days appeared to be far in the rearview mirror.

One last opportunity presented itself. The organizers of the Newport Jazz Festival invited Ellington to perform on the third and final night of the event. The caveat was that festival attendees expected something special, not a rehash of Duke Ellington's classics. Pledging to deliver, the Duke brought his sixteen-piece band, filled with saxophonists, trumpeters, and of course himself.

Rebirth at Fifty-Seven

Duke Ellington in his fourth decade as a pianist and bandleader

Opening Act

Roughly seven thousand jazz buffs were on the grassy lawns of Newport's Freebody Park on July 7, 1956. Some were children of the rich and famous—those who owned nearby mansions—while others were jazz lovers who had traveled a long distance. The jazz festival was in its third year, and it promised great things for the future.

Duke Ellington and his famous orchestra came onstage at 8:00 p.m. With some members of the band missing, they started with a rendition of "The Star-Spangled Banner" that left most listeners unimpressed. Ellington followed with two other songs, but he and his musicians then left the stage, opening the way for three successive performances by other groups. This had all been planned, but it seemed to some audience members that the Duke had already come and gone and Newport would be his last show. Confirming that feeling was the presence of Voice of America recording machines, which would record the concert for radio. If the Duke did nothing worthy on this night, all the world would know it.

Slightly more than three hours passed, during which the other bands received moderate applause. The festival was winding down, and though there had been good moments, it was not the great success that the promoters hoped for. Newspaper and magazine correspondents watched Duke Ellington for clues: Could the Duke summon his old magic? Or would he go off quietly into the night?

A reporter for *Time* magazine noted that "onstage famed Bandleader Duke Ellington, a trace of coldness rimming his urbanity, refused to recognize the fact."[1] When Ellington and his musicians came back for their second

Rebirth at Fifty-Seven

The Newport Jazz Festival put Duke Ellington and his beleaguered band back on top.

Newport Jazz Festival Performers

While the 1956 Newport Jazz Festival represented a turn in fortune for Duke Ellington, he and his band were hardly the only musicians there. The Bud Shank Quartet, Chico Hamilton, and Chicago veteran Anita O'Day (whose performance at the 1958 Newport Jazz Festival would go on to be featured in the documentary *Jazz on a Summer's Day*) were all much higher on the musical charts than Duke Ellington was at the time. Virtually everyone knew, however, that there had been a time—even a decade earlier—when they would have had to settle for second billing below the Duke.

set—this time, with all of the band members present and accounted for—it was 11:45 p.m., and people were already headed for the exits.

Ellington started with one of his surefire favorites. "Take the A Train" was written fifteen years earlier, but it remained Duke Ellington's signature song. There was no magic in the song this night, however. Ellington followed with two other renditions of old favorites, and the audience dropped by nearly a quarter. There was dew on the Newport grass, and people wanted to get home.

The Duke had one last card to play. He announced his men would play "Diminuendo and Crescendo in Blue." It was another of the famous Ellington hits, written in 1938. Recognizing the song's worth, some concert goers stayed a bit longer. "A strange, spasmodic air, that carried memories of wilderness and city, rose through the salt-scented air like a fire on a beach," *Time* magazine declared. "Minutes passed. People turned back from the exits; snoozers woke up. All at once the promise of new excitement revived the dying evening."[2]

Ellington's men gave it their all, but the performance of the tenor saxophonist made all the difference. Massachusetts-born Paul Gonsalves was a relatively new band member. He did not have the gravitas, or endurance, of older band members. But on this particular night, he let rip a saxophone solo that went on for 26 repeats (each of them slightly varied).

Gradually, the beat began to ricochet from the audience as more and more fans began to clap hands on the offbeats until the crowd was one vast, rhythmic chorus, yelling its approval. There were howls of "More! More!" and there was dancing in the aisles. One young woman broke loose from her escort and danced solo around the field, while a young man encouraged her by shouting, 'Go, go, go!'"[3]

This platinum blonde in a black dress turned out to be Elaine Anderson, a socialite who was expected to act in demure, calm fashion. Instead, she spontaneously burst into music-inspired joy, and in doing so she ignited the entire audience. The festival wound down around 2:00 a.m., and by that late hour, Duke Ellington's career was reborn. For the rest of his life, the Duke would quip that he was a very young fellow—that he was born at Newport in the summer of 1956.

A Coveted Honor

Ellington had won many honors over the previous three decades. One that eluded him was a cover of *Time* magazine, which was (and is) a particular badge of recognition. The jazz legend, and Ellington's contemporary, Benny Goodman had been featured more than a decade previous. But Duke Ellington finally had his glorious moment. Just a month after the Newport Jazz Festival, his handsome, but also weary, face was featured on the cover. The magazine article highlighted Ellington's physical and professional restoration:

> The man who is responsible for this remarkable musical idiom is a tall (6 ft 1 inch), rangy (185 lbs.) fellow whose newfound trimness parallels his re-discovered energies. His habitual expression combines curiosity, mockery and humor. In his pleasant Harlem apartment or in his dressing

room, he usually goes about in shorts, possibly to preserve his 100-plus suits of clothes.[4]

How had Duke Ellington reignited his career at the age of fifty-seven? That question was easier to answer than its corollary: How had a middle-class African American man risen from obscure circumstances to become the most famous bandleader in America?

Chapter 2

A Capital Time

Born near the end of the nineteenth century, Duke Ellington grew up in America's capital city, Washington, DC. From his earliest years, he was accustomed to seeing grand sights, but with this experience came the bittersweet knowledge that he—and other black citizens—were not allowed to savor or enjoy all of them.

At the turn of the twentieth century, Washington, DC, had one of the largest African American populations in the nation; roughly one-third of the city's residents were black. However, this did not mean African Americans were welcome to the major events. One of the most striking examples of the segregation practiced in DC was the opening and dedication of the Lincoln Memorial in 1922. Though Abraham Lincoln was famous for having emancipated the slaves—the ancestors of a sizable number of DC's population—not a single black face appears in the photographs of the dedication ceremony.

The young Duke Ellington knew about segregation firsthand. But he came from a family and a section of

16 DUKE ELLINGTON: Legendary Composer and Bandleader

Duke Ellington grew up in Washington, DC, when the US capital looked more like a southern city than a northern one.

A Capital Time

African American society that did not linger on the issue. Throughout his life, Ellington preferred to dwell on the positive aspects and brush off the unpleasant ones. When people asked about his youth in Washington, DC, the Duke usually made a pun, saying it had been a "capital" time.

A Blessed Beginning

James Edward Ellington and Daisy Kennedy were married on January 3, 1898. James Ellington was the son of working-class black parents who had already done a good deal to improve their social and economic status, particularly by relocating from rural North Carolina to Washington, DC. Daisy Kennedy was a multiracial young woman of both African and Cherokee descent, the daughter of two former slaves. Her father, James William Kennedy, was a member of the Metropolitan police, one of only forty African Americans on the payroll in 1910.

Daisy Kennedy regarded herself as one or even two steps above her husband in social and economic grace, but this did not deter the couple from coming together. They tragically lost their first baby during childbirth, so when their second child, Edward Kennedy Ellington (his nickname of "Duke" would come later), came into the world on April 29, 1899, they were overjoyed. Though he could hardly be expected to remember this momentous occasion, Duke Ellington described his birth and his parents thusly:

> They were a wonderful, compatible couple, and God blessed their marriage with a fine baby boy (eight pounds, eight ounces). They raised him, nurtured him, coddled him, and spoiled him. They raised him in the palm of the hand and gave him everything they thought he wanted. Finally, when he was about seven or eight, they let his feet touch the ground.[1]

Ellington's assessment of his parents' behavior and treatment of him was all too accurate. As the only boy in the family—and for many years the only child—he was fussed over and doted upon by his mother, father, and all manner of relatives.

> So I was pampered and pampered, and spoiled rotten by all the women in the family, aunts and cousins, but my mother never took her eyes off precious little me, her jewel, until I was four years old, when I proceeded to the front lawn with some authority to examine the rosebushes, stumbled over the lawn-mower, fell on a piece of a broken milk bottle, and cut the fourth finger of my left hand.[2]

Worried for her son's safety, Daisy Kennedy Ellington summoned not one but two doctors. Her concern over her only child was profound, but this was also the time when her belief in God—already apparent—became stronger. She imparted this same belief to her son, her most famous words being "Edward, you are blessed. You don't have anything to worry about. Edward, you are blessed!"[3]

There is a forced quality to the words, an insistence that suggests the mother was not completely certain. What we are sure of is that the young Ellington absorbed her message. For most of his life, Duke Ellington believed that he sailed under a lucky star, that divine providence was looking out for him. To be sure, many children hear similar words from their parents. But in the Duke's case, it became a mantra and an endless source of comfort. Church attendance, and the extended Ellington-Kennedy family, were clearly at the center of Duke Ellington's life. But from about the age of twelve, he was also a boy of the streets, seeking to become a man.

Discovering Music and Maturity

Washington, DC, especially the northwest section, abounded in clubs, piano bars, and pool halls—and Duke Ellington sneaked into a fair number of them. Daisy Kennedy Ellington and her religious faith provided one stable pillar of her son's life and emotional makeup. Duke Ellington's father, whom he frequently described as a gentleman and charmer—quick with a compliment or flattery—provided another.

Was the Duke a precocious boy where the opposite sex was concerned? Later in life, at unguarded moments, he said he was a girl-crazy teenager. Ellington's fascination with the opposite sex did not diminish with age. Rather, it was one of the defining elements of his personality.

Two Churches

In his autobiography, *Music Is My Mistress*, Duke Ellington revealed that as a child, his family actually were parishioners at two different churches. His pious mother brought him to Nineteenth Street Baptist, and the two would join his father for services at John Wesley A.M.E. Zion. Though it is difficult to tell whether this was simply the result of extreme religiosity on his mother's part or proof of a marital mismatch between mother and father, there were signs that pointed to the Ellington marriage being a troubled one. The Duke usually glossed over his parents' differences, and in one sense he was accurate. They loved him, adored him, and made him feel exceptionally special.

But women were not the only interest beginning to flower during Duke Ellington's adolescence. Earlier in his life, Ellington had formal piano lessons, but they left almost no mark upon him. Now, he was fascinated by the informal music he heard in beer and pool halls:

> There was one great poolroom on T Street, between Sixth and Seventh N.W., Frank Holliday's poolroom, next to the Howard Theatre…Guys from all walks of life seemed to converge there: school kids over and under sixteen; college students and graduates, some starting out in law and medicine and science;

A Capital Time

Washington's nightlife held a special fascination for Ellington.

and lots of Pullman porters and dining-car waiters. These last had much to say about the places they'd been. The names of the cities would be very impressive. You would hear them say, "I just left Chicago," or "Last night I was in Cleveland."[4]

Did Duke Ellington suspect that he would be one of these travelers one day? Or that his career as a traveling bandleader would be connected intimately with Pullman cars? We cannot say for certain. But it does seem that a spirit of adventure filled him from an early age.

Chapter 3

A Medley of Music

Even in our own time, when a person can summon songs and sounds on the internet with just the stroke of a key, it is difficult to capture the precise excitement and vitality of the Jazz Age. The spellings at the time varied, with some people calling it "jass," others naming it "jasz," and still others calling it "jazz," but the sound remained the same—a brilliant but also haunting evocation of the human condition. For his part, Duke Ellington did not set out to find jazz. The music found him.

An Impressive Predecessor

Ragtime was all the rage at the start of the twentieth century, but its force was spent by about the year 1915. With a lively and "ragged" rhythm, ragtime was an intensely exuberant new sound, one made available to the masses. Until about the year 1890, music was primarily an upper-class pursuit, with African Americans and working-class white citizens getting by with folk music (most of which was never printed or published). Ragtime allowed a

Musician Scott Joplin became known as the "King of Ragtime" after composing several ragtime hits, including "The Entertainer."

number of African Americans in the door to an established musical scene, however, and jazz went further: the door was practically broken down:

> On May 13, 1915, a five-piece white group from New Orleans arrived in Chicago for a six-week engagement at the basement restaurant at Randolph and Clark, called Lamb's Café. They billed themselves as "Brown's Band from Dixieland," after their trombonist…The kind of music they played was already growing familiar in black neighborhoods of the city, but most white Chicagoans had never heard anything like it.[1]

Jazz was a rural sound that won great fame when it came to the cities. It was as different from classical European music as can be imagined. White musicians did some of the front work, bringing the sound to segregated venues in New York and Chicago, but once it arrived, jazz was performed with great skill and ingenuity by African American bands and musicians. The most well known at the time was James Reese Europe.

Born in the South but raised in Washington, DC, James Reese Europe was an extraordinary talent. He brought jazz to the halls where classical music was usually played, and he made jazz seem the most exciting new art form since anyone could remember. Handsome and bespectacled, Europe was the essence of the serious black musician. He did just fine by 1915, but the advent of the Great War—also known as World War I—truly catapulted him to fame.

In 1914, nearly all the European powers went to war in the conflict that we now call the First World War. The

United States remained aloof and stayed out of the war until April 1917, when President Woodrow Wilson declared that America would fight to keep the world "safe for democracy."

Black Americans experienced a variety of emotions when called upon to serve in World War I. Many were pleased and proud to do so, to serve the flag that had led the Union to victory in 1865 and that had witnessed the end of slavery. Other African Americans decried the entire effort, however. As bad as Kaiser Wilhelm and Imperial Germany were, the United States was not that much better, they declared. Why fight for Uncle Sam in a European war when racist laws keeping blacks as second-class citizens were on the books in most states of the nation?

James Reese Europe was among those who were proud to serve. Joining the New York Fifteenth Regiment, he witnessed the change to the "Harlem Hellfighters," the single most successful black combat force in World War I. Europe was a captain in the regiment but also its bandleader, and he

A Medley of Music 27

In addition to serving on the battlefield, James Reese Europe (*far left*) led the Harlem Hellfighters Regimental Band during World War I.

brought his unique new sound to Paris and other parts of France. By the time the Harlem Hellfighters came home in 1919, they were heroes, and jazz was better known to millions of people.

Despite being part of a major military victory and forging an entirely new musical genre, James Reese Europe's seemingly bright future was not to be. In 1919, the same year he and the Harlem regiment returned from France, Europe was killed in an almost inexplicable act of violence. After getting into an argument with one of his drummers, the band member stabbed Europe in the neck. While Europe waved off any serious concerns about the injury, he was taken to a hospital. Despite their best efforts, doctors were unable to stop the blood loss, and James Europe died.

At the time of James Reese Europe's death, there was no obvious replacement, no black musician who could take up his mantle. But others were waiting in the wings, and some of them aspired to be the new Jim Europe. Duke Ellington was one of them.

A Duke Gets Serious

As he headed into his middle teen years, Ellington seemed to have a greater talent for athletics than for music. His early piano lessons had been a failure, and he showed more interest in baseball than cultural events. His nickname Duke came from high school friends who were impressed with his fine clothes and personal style. In an interview, one of his cousins revealed that Duke took his nickname to heart:

> He used to come to get his dinner and he would say, "You know Mother, I'm going to be one of

the greatest men in the world." And she used to say, "Oh, Boy, hush your mouth." He'd say "Yes, I am." Then he would kiss her when she would be scolding him. And he would say, "Everybody in the world is going to call me Duke Ellington. I'm ze Duke, ze grand and ze glorious Duke." We used to laugh, it was so funny. He predicted his future. Everybody in the whole world did call him Duke. He said, "I'm going to bow before kings and queens." *And he did that, too.*[2]

Though he clearly felt destined for greatness, it wasn't until attending a piano recital that the Duke began to take music seriously. While he had fallen under the spell of jazz as he covertly listened in pool halls, this more age-appropriate experience affected him just as deeply.

At the age of fourteen, Duke Ellington spent an extended summer vacation in New Jersey. Friends took him to Philadelphia to observe the piano playing of Harvey Brooks, an African American youngster only a bit older than himself. Duke was struck by the elegance and power with which Brooks clicked the keys, and he was hooked. He intended to play as well and fluently as Brooks, even though his earlier music lessons had failed. Friends were quick to point out another motive, however. Duke saw that pretty girls came to admire the sophisticated fellow on the piano bench, and that didn't hurt, either. Soon, Duke, too, would be stunning audiences.

Though he excelled at mechanical drawing at Armstrong Technical High School, ultimately, the lure of music and the adult world proved too strong. Duke Ellington chose not to continue his education. He left high school without his diploma and plunged right into the hard work of making a living and supporting a family while the United States was still engaged in the First World War. He made his first money as a painter of signs and a message runner for the Treasury Department. That so many young men were in Europe, fighting Germany, made his path smoother. To his own surprise, music offered a better venue than almost any other. Of the different roles he took on, Duke Ellington was happiest as a bandleader.

Chapter 4

Leader of the Band

The earliest photograph of a Duke Ellington band dates from the year 1920. An indoor scene greets the viewer, who sees the handsome and tall Duke Ellington at the center. He is seated, but his long legs and massive hands stand out. To the right is the female singer and her husband. To the left is an unidentified woman and the drummer, Sonny Greer.

Anyone willing to spend times in attics, basements, and flea markets can find photographs like this one. They were everywhere in the early 1920s, a time when hundreds of small-time bands suddenly emerged. But the difference of the "Duke's Serenaders," as he called them, is obvious. Though he was surrounded by talented musicians, the Duke ran the show. His sophisticated ear and commanding physical presence shaped the band's direction.

Playing by Ear

Duke Ellington never described exactly how he came to possess such a good musical ear. He had little formal training, and even late in his career, his sketch notes sometimes resembled a mess. However, there was no doubt

32 DUKE ELLINGTON: Legendary Composer and Bandleader

At twenty, Duke Ellington already knew how to hold center stage.

Leader of the Band 33

that he could hear a tune and almost immediately figure out how to use it to its full potential.

If Ellington's formal musical training was limited to a few dozen hours, his informal apprenticeships lasted only a year or two. He described his tutors in this way:

> Doc Perry wore glasses and looked very much like the kids try to look today...He was respected by musicians, show people, and the laymen as well. Doc was an impressive sight no matter what he was doing, and in spite of his own masterly digital dexterity, he respected any musician, school or ear. He felt that if the composer wrote it that way, then that's the way the composer would like it played.[1]

Though Oliver "Doc" Perry likely helped Ellington refine his talent, one cannot give him credit for Ellington's natural ability. A musical ear can be improved, but a supremely good one is usually a gift that one is born with. One either "hears" the timing and the tempo or does not. What can be said with some certainty is that Ellington already demonstrated this gift by the time he turned twenty-one.

Opening Moves

In the spring of 1919, Duke Ellington advertised his band as for hire in the Washington, DC, phonebook. The Duke's Serenaders would perform syncopated music for discriminating ears, he declared, and the band played at least twice that season (one of their concerts ran four long hours). By now, Duke Ellington had written a handful of songs, most of which have since been lost to memory. One of the few that survives is "What You Gonna Do When the Bed Breaks Down?"

"Jazz" is now spelled with two *z*'s, but originally it was spelled with two *s*'s, and the word itself became closely associated with sex. As a musical genre, jazz touched on other topics, including money, race, and social station, but sex and love were its major themes. Duke Ellington's music, and the compositions played by the Duke's Serenaders, was no exception to the rule.

The Start of a Family

Edna Thompson grew up in the same neighborhood as Duke Ellington, and the two met at Armstrong Technical High School. She came from a family at least one rung higher on the socio-economic scale, but this never seems to have gotten in the way of their affection. When Edna became pregnant, the high school sweethearts decided to marry. Mercer Kennedy Ellington was born eight months later.

Duke Ellington did not exactly relish his new role as a father. Through music, he was already earning a decent living, and it was not long before he purchased a home for the three-member family. But Duke Ellington was just

> ## Sex in the 1920s
> Americans of the early 1900s were not especially puritanical, and sexual activity—both within and outside of marriage—was common. But World War I made a powerful difference: Many servicemen, black and white alike, came home with exotic experiences and a desire for more. Then, too, the rather sudden availability of birth control allowed for a major change. We have no firm statistics on which to rely, but the anecdotal record suggests that Americans' attitude toward sex changed more in the 1920s than in any prior decade. Only the 1960s would equal it.

beginning his career as a musician, and he resented having to spend time at home with his wife and baby boy. Before long, he spent more time outside of the house than in.

Edna Thompson Ellington later remembered this period with sadness. Though she knew he was a man of music, she had not anticipated just how strong the hold of his "mistress" would be. There were few fights; rather, the couple simply drifted apart.

During this time, Duke Ellington's contact with his parents also began to diminish. Just a few years prior, in 1915, Daisy and James Ellington had another child, Ruth Ellington. But as little time as he had for his own wife and son, Duke Ellington had even less for his parents and new sister. He was a man on the move, and though he gave

36   DUKE ELLINGTON: Legendary Composer and Bandleader

In New York, Ellington added Sonny Greer, known as "the Sweet-Singing Drummer," to his orchestra.

profound lip service to his parents, the only thing he seemed to have time for was music.

The Home of Jazz

Duke Ellington spent the first three years of his music career entirely in Washington, DC. The capital city afforded him plenty of opportunity, and he moved from strength to strength. But by 1923, he felt blocked—denied the very best venue of them all.

So the Duke and his musicians set off for New York City for the first time. Where they stayed and even where they played remain a mystery, but there is no doubt that they profited from the experience. New York City in general, and Harlem in particular, was entering a renaissance that ranged from the written and spoken word to music and visual arts. The Jazz Age had been born, and black artists

A Gentle Touch

Duke Ellington sometimes employed as many as twenty musicians at one time. He had a great fondness for his crew, and he seldom fired or even laid anyone off. The Duke's bank account varied considerably, but he continued to pay his players, rain or shine.

The Duke also became a master at handling his musicians, some of whom were quite temperamental. Discipline was rare. Harsh words were seldom uttered. Instead, the Duke managed his musicians with the lightest and gentlest of touches. They, in turn, came to respect his eccentricities. One of these revolved around sleep. Duke Ellington seldom rose before noon, and even then it often required a great amount of effort to rouse him.

were flourishing. One saw it everywhere—on the streets of Manhattan, on the public beaches, and in the concert halls. But the African American nightclubs of Harlem demonstrated the greatest variety of all. The richness of talent inspired Duke Ellington to evolve and grow his band.

"It was at the Kentucky Club that our music acquired new colors and characteristics," Duke later wrote. "First we added Charlie Irvis, a trombone player nicknamed 'Plug' because of the unusual mute he used. Then, when Artie Whetsol went back to Washington to continue his studies at Howard University, we got Bubber Miley, the epitome of soul and a master with the plunger mute…Sonny Greer was in his element here, and he was known as The Sweet-Singing Drummer."[2]

The excitement was palpable. But the Duke Ellington Band (not yet known as the Orchestra) was still one of dozens. There was no reason to expect that this particular band would soar past the competition.

The Cotton Club made all the difference.

Chapter 5

Sudden Fame

Though they had played in New York during the early 1920s, it wasn't until December 1927 that the Duke Ellington Orchestra made its first appearance at the Cotton Club, generally regarded as the most exciting venue in all of New York City during the Harlem Renaissance. What could have been a booking limited to a week or ten days turned into a months-long run of performances. Duke Ellington—and his orchestra—suddenly became famous.

Black Musicians, White Patrons

In 1927, Harlem had any number of clubs, bars, or speakeasies. Just as Harlem had become a center for the printed word, with the publication of books such as *The New Negro*—a collection of fiction and essays by African American writers—the community had also become the beating heart of the new, exciting music known as jazz. Even so, when the Cotton Club opened in 1926, it was like a revelation. People flocked from all parts of Manhattan and its suburbs. Most of them were white.

Sudden Fame

The Cotton Club became a symbol of New York sophistication and the Harlem music scene's vitality.

The Cotton Club employed many bouncers. They winked when famous black men and women, such as the singer Paul Robeson, entered, but most black people were simply barred at the door. The vast majority of the patrons were white. The musicians were mostly black. Even against this strange backdrop of distinction and discrimination, the Cotton Club exemplified the musical aspect of the Harlem Renaissance.

Duke Ellington and his musicians came to the stage for the first time on December 4, 1927. They played "Creole Love Call," their newest number. This rousing song led to many others, and the crowd responded with enthusiasm. In a matter of weeks, the Duke Ellington Orchestra had become the hottest thing in New York music.

The Ellington Style

Up to the year 1927, Duke Ellington was one of several talented black musicians trying to make the grade. But within a few months of his first Cotton Club appearance, the Duke took on a new persona. Ellington had long been a crowd pleaser, but his musicians were doing just as much of the work. By 1928, he developed the Ellington style, which involved dramatic flourishes on the piano. Ellington's fingers pounded the piano, but then soared into the air. This was showmanship at its very best.

Ellington's personal style also became more pronounced. His habits had never been very regular, but he now made a virtue out of nonconformity and noncompliance. Ellington rose as late as possible, dined on the same food—steak, fries, and salad—almost every day, and put off writing the

Joe "King" Oliver led the Creole Jazz Band through the 1920s.

A Stolen Song

While "Creole Love Call" might have been a watershed musical number for Duke Ellington's career, there's a shadow over that first performance at the Cotton Club. It wasn't his song. Duke Ellington and his band recorded "Creole Love Call" earlier in 1927, but the melody was remarkably similar to a song called "Camp Meeting Blues," composed by Joe "King" Oliver with his group, the Creole Jazz Band. In the course of a lawsuit, it became apparent that Ellington's saxophonist Rudy Jackson had plagiarized the melody, representing it as his original work. While Joe Oliver's lawsuit ultimately failed since he couldn't present the proper paperwork establishing his copyright for "Camp Meeting Blues," Ellington took immediate action: he fired Rudy Jackson.

conclusion to his songs for as long as possible. One of his biographers expressed it thus:

> He was the most chronic of procrastinators, a man who never did today what he could put off until next month, or next year. He left letters unanswered, contracts unsigned, watches unworn, and longtime companions unwed, and the only thing harder than getting him out of bed in the afternoon was getting him to finish writing a new piece of music in time for the premiere.[1]

How did he get away with it?

Ellington's incredible talent provides one-third of the answer, and his amazing charm gives yet another. Easygoing beyond the norm, Ellington could win forgiveness from almost anyone. But there was still another part to the Ellington formula. He got away with chronic procrastination by using it as a means to "lift," or steal, from his own musicians, exploiting their gifts to make up for his lack of preparation. This is a hard thing to say about a great musical talent, but there is no doubt Ellington milked the men of his orchestra. He often came to practice with his ideas and composition only half-finished. During that final performance, he lifted musical bars and melodies from the sounds of his musicians.

Why did the musicians not call Ellington out? This is another of the great questions from this era. Charm and friendship provide most of the answer. Ellington was deeply loyal to the men of his orchestra, often keeping them on the payroll long after their best musical years were over. He won over his musicians time after time. On those rare occasions when a major conflict brewed, Ellington usually headed it off.

Only one thing threatened the continued rise of the band. The Great Depression struck in the autumn of 1929.

A National Crisis

For nearly a decade, the United States had enjoyed unprecedented prosperity. The profits from new products such as automobiles, radios, and air conditioners allowed the consumer public to get what it wanted, including entertainment. One reason Duke Ellington and his band did so well from 1927 to 1929 was the amount of money the average patron had in his or her pocket. This all came crashing down with the fall of the stock market in 1929.

Duke Ellington was philosophical about the economic crash and financial reversal. He had already done better than his butler father and his policeman grandfather. But the band entailed large expenses, and Ellington was concerned. Fortunately, he had a backer. This was Irving Mills, one of the biggest impresarios of the time.

Born in New York City, Irving Mills was five years older than Duke Ellington. A hard-nosed person possessed with incredible drive, Mills fastened on the music business, but he could have sold, swapped, or traded almost any commodity. A fast-talking promoter, Mills knew a good thing when he saw it, and Duke Ellington's band was as good as they came.

The agreements that Mills and Ellington signed were almost always in the former's favor. Duke Ellington did virtually all the work and often ended up with only 25 percent of the receipts. Ellington was careful not to

46 DUKE ELLINGTON: Legendary Composer and Bandleader

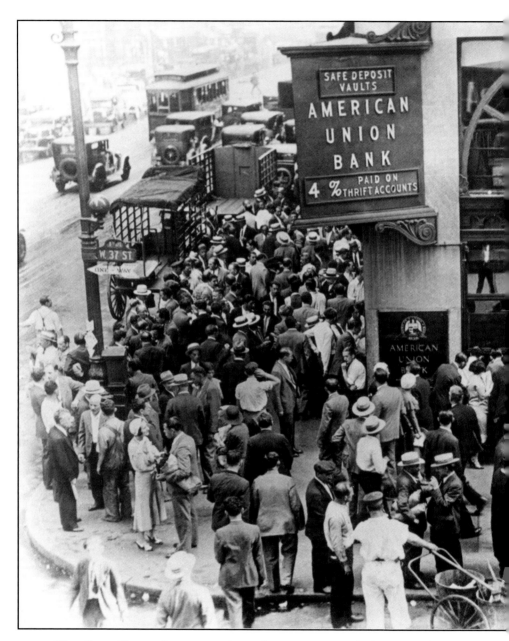

The Great Depression was a time of severe economic hardship for everyone, including artists and musicians.

Sudden Fame 47

complain in public, however; he knew it was a fortunate entertainer who could make it through the Great Depression. The music business of the 1930s was every bit as cutthroat as the one we know today. If Duke Ellington had more time, he might have been able to sort out the contracts, performance dates, and so forth. But the Big Band era was all about volume, meaning that Ellington needed to perform almost every night.

It made perfect sense for Ellington to turn the business management over to Irving Mills. Later in life, Ellington expressed some regrets about the decision. But the chances are that, without a capable and aggressive business manager like Mills, his band would have folded in the 1930s. So when Mills proposed that Ellington take the band to England, the Duke practically jumped at the opportunity.

Chapter 6

That Swing

Entertainers and musicians often suffer during economic recessions and depressions. Many of their former clientele cannot afford to go out to shows. On the other hand, the desire for entertainment, if only to avoid one's troubles for a few hours, becomes even more profound during times of financial struggle. Though Duke Ellington and his orchestra lost some devoted fans during the 1930s, those they kept became hooked for life.

Hitting His Stride

In 1931, Duke Ellington recorded one of the best-known and most popular of all his songs, "It Don't Mean a Thing (If It Ain't Got That Swing)." With a rollicking piano arrangement and a robust showing from the Duke's trombone player, Joe Nanton, the song truly defined swing—a full three years before the "Swing Era" officially began. This song was clearly Ellington's best to date, and the instrumentals showed his band to be among the most innovative in the business. Now considered a jazz classic, it's been covered by numerous bands and artists, including Lady Gaga and Tony Bennett.

How good was the Duke Ellington Orchestra in 1932? This question has been posed by many music critics as well as historians. The consensus is that the Duke was miles ahead of his jazz competition, that his compositions were more advanced, and that the orchestra was a smooth-running machine. Only Benny Goodman's band came close to equaling the Duke's talent and success.

Born in Chicago in 1909, clarinet player and bandleader Benny Goodman was a decade younger than Duke Ellington. Goodman's talent was just as profound as the Duke's, however, and by the mid-1930s, his band was receiving just as many rave reviews. One way Ellington kept some distance between himself and Goodman was through his triumphal visit to Great Britain, in the summer of 1933.

A Trip Across the Atlantic

Duke Ellington maintained all sorts of superstitions. Generally, he was opposed to ocean travel. But since there was no commercial air travel in 1933, the S.S. *Olympic* was the only way for the Duke Ellington Orchestra to make it across the pond to England.

Several days at sea persuaded Ellington that ocean liner travel was not terrible. Arriving in London, he encountered other obstacles, including the question of where African American musicians could stay because some hotels simply refused to admit black guests. But when Ellington found a place at the Dorchester Hotel, in Mayfair, he commenced a lifelong love affair with London and its people.

50 DUKE ELLINGTON: Legendary Composer and Bandleader

The Duke Ellington Orchestra at the height of its success, around 1935

Benny Goodman (*left*) was one of the few bandleaders who could match Duke Ellington's talent.

The English were different, Ellington declared. No matter how upper class or snooty they might have appeared, the English responded to genuine talent. And he clearly had the knack for making new friends.

When the Duke and his orchestra opened at the Palladium, they played to a sold-out theater. Louis Armstrong had been there a year prior, and other black musicians were starting to appear on the London scene. But none did so with Ellington's flair. Perhaps his success stemmed from the charm he inherited from his father and social graces impressed upon him by his mother. Then again, he may have picked them up in Harlem from his compatriots. In either case, Ellington came across as the perfect, consummate gentleman, and he succeeded with the English—upper, middle, and lower class alike. When he and his band were broadcast on the BBC (British Broadcasting Corporation), the Duke was an immediate hit.

Only the English critics held back. Some, like the *London Times*, damned Ellington with faint praise, while others criticized him as an imitator. But the small circles of jazz enthusiasts took to Ellington, declaring his music the finest they ever heard. After fifty days in England, the Duke took his musicians to France. Their time there was short, but it was the start of yet another love affair. Ellington made fast friends in London and Paris, and he kept many of them for the rest of his long life.

It was also on the London trip that Ellington showed off his band's finest vocal talent. The Duke Ellington Orchestra was known for its instrumentalists, and the music, rather than words. But in jazz singer Ivie Anderson, Ellington found his best voice. Though she sometimes had a rough

Ellington and the English

London has long been a favorable place for African American entertainers. The first of all black thespians, Ira Aldridge, left Baltimore for England in the 1820s. But Duke Ellington seemed to jibe with the English better than almost any other black entertainer. In part, this was thanks to his immaculate style and that of his musicians. Ellington also had something else: a gentle and ironic sense of humor that the English adored. While some claimed Louis Armstrong was the greater African American talent, most English—even the critics—asserted that Ellington was the most enjoyable and affable of the black entertainers.

presence off the stage (including verbal abuse aimed at her boss), onstage, however, Ivie Anderson displayed great sex appeal and a powerful voice that appealed to audiences on both sides of the Atlantic. Though Ellington did not realize it, his orchestra was approaching a level of perfection, one that he maintained for several glorious years.

Coping with Loss

Duke Ellington was in rare form at the beginning of 1935. His band—commonly referred to as the Duke Ellington

That Swing 55

Ivie Anderson was the most renowned—and admired—of all Ellington's female vocalists.

Orchestra—was in great demand. But this was also a time of severe personal loss.

Daisy Kennedy Ellington was diagnosed with cancer. Her son had her moved from Washington, DC, to Michigan, where she received some of the best possible treatment. But all the doctors' efforts failed, and she died in June 1935.

Reeling from his mother's death, the Duke went into a tailspin. Friends were not certain he would recover. Ellington had long lived by his mother's maxim, that he was blessed, but his mother's demise put this in doubt. At this time, Ellington began to wear a gold cross, which he was seldom thereafter seen without. But neither the Duke's friends nor the music critics were surprised that he managed to develop a song out of his misery.

"Reminiscing in Tempo" came straight from Duke Ellington's grief. Very likely, it would have taken him longer to emerge from that grief if he didn't have his music to channel his emotions. In "Reminiscing in Tempo," gone is the infectious and joyful rhythm of songs like "If It Ain't Got That Swing." In its place is a slower, softer, and sadder use of the orchestra's strings and trumpets. Running twelve minutes long, the song has an inescapable sorrow, even in its more impassioned moments. The song was regarded as his best since 1931. But Ellington's grief was soon compounded by the loss of his father.

James Edward Ellington had been a hard drinker for many years. At times, he covered it well, and at other times it seemed he would drown in his alcoholism. He made a late attempt to dry out but died from cancer in 1937. The Duke did not have as much to say about his father's death.

Beyond the shadow of a doubt, he was closer to his mother. But the loss of his father very likely still weighed on him. The fairy tale he told others—as well as himself—came to an end in the mid-1930s. He had lost both of his parents and now had to stand on his own. Ellington still considered himself "blessed," but he was not undamaged.

Chapter 7

Top of the World

As World War II approached, many Americans experienced a sense of dread. They remembered World War I and the hardships that had arisen from a global war. A significant percentage of Americans wished to stay out of the new conflict, which was brewing on the horizon.

The year 1939 was the dividing line, the year when war broke out in Europe. In Duke Ellington's life, there was another schism forming. Irving Mills had been Ellington's business manager for more than a decade. In that time, the Duke had made a good deal of money, but Mills and his company earned far more. After examining the books, Duke Ellington decided to end the partnership. For years to come, he would be his own business manager, for better or worse.

Though it was undoubtedly a time of turmoil, 1939 was also the year that Duke Ellington and his band returned to

Top of the World 59

In 1939, Duke Ellington and his orchestra headed back to Europe.

Europe. They arrived in the winter, late enough to sense the dreaded onset of war, but just early enough to carry out their mission. The European tour was a success, but not a smash like that of its 1933 predecessor. The Duke and his orchestra won consistently good reviews, but there was a sense that they were now *one* of the best, instead of the top band among European listeners. However, the Duke had an ace up his sleeve, and he revealed it that same year.

The ace was none other than the Duke's other self: the pianist and composer Billy Strayhorn.

The Kid Genius

Born in Ohio in 1915, Billy Strayhorn came from a fractured home and endured a painful upbringing. He had none of Duke Ellington's confidence or magnetism. But on the level of sheer talent, he was just about as good as the Duke, who was smart enough to see that talent and harness it for his own purpose.

Strayhorn met Duke Ellington in the winter of 1939—just days before the orchestra was to leave for its European tour. Legend has it that Strayhorn went to the piano to play "Sophisticated Lady" and that he did so just about as well as Ellington himself. Strayhorn then added some variations on the song and played it to an astonished Ellington, who then gave Strayhorn directions to his Harlem home. Their second meeting had to wait until the European tour was over, but that encounter would prove to be the beginning of something rare and magnificent—the collaboration of two musical geniuses at the height of their composing power.

Strayhorn was paid only a handful of dollars in the first year of their association, and there was no doubt as to who was senior and junior. But Strayhorn composed the song that became the Duke Ellington Orchestra signature tune in 1941: "Take the A Train."

Top of the World 61

Talented pianist and indispensable band member Billy Strayhorn (*left*) composed the now-legendary "Take the A Train."

An Express Train to the Top

When Billy Strayhorn wrote "Take the A Train," passenger trains were at the height of their popularity and use. Sung with great power and skill by vocalist Ivie Anderson, the words brought images of a fast-moving train, carrying passengers from the central and southern parts of New York City to Sugar Hill, where Duke Ellington resided. (One of the earliest formal recordings of the song was performed inside of a commuter train, with the entire Duke Ellington Orchestra in attendance.)

For present-day New Yorkers, these commuter trains remain a necessity as they travel around the city for both work and pleasure. But the song is about more than mere transportation. The A train was, and remains, an express subway train that can take commuters from downtown Manhattan all the way up to Harlem. For Strayhorn and the Duke Ellington Orchestra, Harlem was the center of the action—the beating heart of New York's music scene. Anyone interested in experiencing the most vital part of New York in the 1930s and '40s would have undoubtedly hopped on the A train and headed uptown.

Jump for Joy

Nineteen forty-one was the year of "Take the A Train" and the year America entered the Second World War. It was also the year Duke Ellington took a major chance: reinventing his orchestra.

Ellington had already performed in several short films, but he had never had the opportunity to "shape" or design any of them. In 1941, Ellington and his musicians spent

The Trains of 1941

There was a noticeable increase in the everyday tempo of American life in 1941. The Second World War had begun in Europe in 1939. America was still on the sidelines, but many people believed the situation would not last for long. There was a significant spike in train traffic that year, and when the United States entered the war—immediately following the Japanese attack on Pearl Harbor—the uptick in transportation was massive. Millions of US servicemen, as well as their wives and sweethearts, were on the move. Billy Strayhorn could not have chosen his time better: "Take the A Train" would become a major hit with the American public.

much time in Southern California, working on the musical revue *Jump for Joy*.

The Duke wanted the revue to showcase the nobler aspects of African American life. In most films and many theatrical productions up until that point, black Americans were portrayed as comic figures, made to seem ridiculous. Ellington brought out his best players for *Jump for Joy*, which premiered in Los Angeles in the summer of 1941.

Ellington had to defend the integrity of the work almost immediately. At an early performance, one of the producers, actor John Garfield, felt that vocalist Herb Jeffries was too light-skinned for the ensemble—and had

64 DUKE ELLINGTON: Legendary Composer and Bandleader

Movie star Mickey Rooney (*center*) stopped by a rehearsal for *Jump for Joy*. Rooney wrote the song "Cymbal Rockin' Sam" for the show.

Top of the World

Jeffries wear makeup to darken the color of his skin. The Duke was furious, feeling that Jeffries was essentially wearing "blackface," recalling exactly the kind of minstrel tradition that Ellington loathed. At the intermission, Jeffries removed the makeup and reappeared in the second half looking more like himself.

The high point of the musical revue was "I Got It Bad (And That Ain't Good)," with singer Ivie Anderson providing sensational delivery. Anderson was already known to tens of thousands of African Americans; it is no exaggeration to say that her name recognition doubled or tripled as a result of *Jump for Joy*.

Initially, *Jump for Joy* earned the Duke Ellington Orchestra a host of rave reviews. Both Charlie Chaplin and Orson Welles, extremely prominent actors and filmmakers, were interested in buying the show and developing it further. But Ellington and his crew weren't interested in handing over the show. This was a revue about black life and identity in America, and they were hardly eager for outside collaborators to come in and rework the show.

Sadly, *Jump for Joy* could not build on its early success. It ran for just nine weeks (122 performances) in California and never had a chance on the New York stage. This was one of Duke Ellington's most painful disappointments, and time after time he looked for a way to resuscitate the revue.

But worse was yet to come.

Band Breakdown

Many Duke Ellington observers believe that 1939–1942 represented the height of his orchestra's success. Not only did he add Billy Strayhorn as the number two composer; Ellington also recruited new talent, such as double bassist Jimmy Blanton and saxophonist Johnny Hodges.

The Ellington sound, as many called it, certainly became unmistakable during this period. Though Benny Goodman was still regarded as the "King of Swing," Ellington drew just as many listeners. But the successes were stopped in their tracks with a string of problems in the winter of 1942. Jimmy Blanton died of tuberculosis in February 1942. Just days later, Ivie Anderson quit the band, saying the asthma that had long plagued her was now unsustainable. She remained in Southern California, where she opened a chicken restaurant.

Clarinetist and saxophone player Barney Bigard left the band about the same time. Though he and the Duke had known each other nearly twenty years, they hardly exchanged a good-bye. It was, in fact, the grimmest of times for Duke Ellington and his orchestra.

It certainly didn't help that Duke Ellington and his musicians endured a punishing schedule, one that would tax the health and strength of younger men. There was no time for complaint: one either moved with the band or fell by the wayside. The health of African American males was, on average, not as good as their white counterparts. Black men suffered disproportionately from several diseases and sicknesses. Tuberculosis felled many black men in the 1940s, but high blood pressure, or hypertension, brought many others low. Duke Ellington did not *seem* to suffer from the complaints of his band members. While physical infirmity didn't seem to be taking a toll, the Duke did have more troubles to face.

Chapter 8

Adversity

While Duke Ellington was too young to serve in the World War I and too old for World War II, this does not mean the war years had no effect on his life and career. Trials and difficulties that had previously been manageable suddenly became even worse. The war years were not good for any of the big band orchestras. They kept at it, performing with great enthusiasm, but something went out of the magic during the hard times of the Second World War.

Black, Brown, and Beige

By 1943, the Duke had mostly won the applause of music critics, both in the United States and Europe. But there was still one piece of praise that they withheld. The critics were nearly unanimous in saying that Ellington was the master at short pieces (particularly three minutes in length)—and that he had yet to show proficiency with longer ones.

Adversity 69

In 1943, the Duke and his orchestra performed *Black, Brown, and Beige* at Carnegie Hall.

Seeking to prove the critics wrong, the Duke composed *Black, Brown, and Beige*, which he and his orchestra played at New York's famed Carnegie Hall in January 1943. Intended as a fund-raiser for the Russian war effort, the concert was a financial success, but a critical flop. Ellington still had not mastered the art of the long piece, the critics declared. Though he was deeply hurt, the Duke passed the matter off with a simple statement, "I guess they didn't dig it."[1]

Duke as Publicity Man

Duke Ellington had always been good at publicity. But as the 1940s passed their midpoint, his skills were more needed than ever. Other big bands were fading or even closing up shop. If Ellington and his musicians were to survive, they had to pull out some new gimmicks.

Ellington was already known for his eccentric behavior, but he intentionally increased the spotlight on himself in the late 1940s. Some music critics wrote more about the Duke and his unusual behavior than about the band's recordings. The critics tended to concentrate on the Duke's hotel and dining habits, as seen in this interview:

Q. What is your best habit?

A. Prayer.

Q. What is your worst habit?

A. Talking too much.

Q. Aside from your usual meal of grapefruit, steak, and vegetables, what would your next favorite meal be?

A. Room service Chinese food—Cantonese.[2]

Some of the Duke's answers seem too swift, right off the cuff, but there is truth lodged in them. He was a creature of habit, continually eating the same food, regardless of which hotel or city he happened to be in. And his habits tended increasingly toward hypochondria.

Earlier in his life, the Duke had been easygoing and laid-back where health was concerned. The deaths of his mother and father—in 1935 and 1937, respectively—left him a changed man. He developed all sorts of odd habits and superstitions, including a hatred of the color brown.

The Duke also developed the habit of phoning his personal physician each day, regardless of where in the world he was. The conversation nearly always began with the same words: "Well, Arthur, how am I feeling today?"[3] Arthur Logan tended to soothe his patient's fears, asking if he had consumed the normal amount of vitamin pills.

What Happened to the Big Bands?

The year 1942 represented the high point for the Big Band era. An entire generation of Americans had grown up with big band music, and as the country entered World War II, they flocked to the nightclubs. However, the end of the World War II came like a thud for the big bands. With the post-war economic boom and cultural shift, many young Americans—including previous big band fans—moved from the cities out to the suburbs, where they could have more space to raise their families. These young couples preferred to listen to big band recordings than to go to see those groups perform live. Then, too, younger Americans preferred solo acts, such as popular singer Frank Sinatra.

But no matter how many pills he took, Ellington remained apprehensive about the state of his health. Then there were other matters to be concerned with: the famous Duke Ellington Orchestra received fewer and fewer listeners with each passing year.

Knowing he was up against a tidal wave of change in musical taste, Duke Ellington continued to play the same music, but he also continually tinkered with new publicity stunts. One of the most successful came in 1950, when he was invited to the White House for a conversation with President Harry S. Truman. Ellington was not the first African American celebrity to be invited to 1600 Pennsylvania Avenue (that distinction went to Frederick Douglass and Booker T. Washington), but he was one of the first black entertainers to be so honored.

The Great James Robbery

Duke Ellington had long been known as a "thief," exploiting the creative talents of his musicians and appropriating his work as their own. But in 1951, the Duke undertook something more visible—and was fortunate to attract more amusement and sardonic laughter than criticism. The "Great James Robbery," as it was called, meant the luring of three new members to the Duke Ellington Orchestra. Trumpeter Harry James was struggling just as much with finding work for his band, and things got markedly more difficult when Duke Ellington hired away three of James's musicians: trombone player Juan Tizol, drummer Louie Bellson, and alto saxophonist Willie Smith. The addition of these members helped the quality of the act but couldn't altogether revive the band.

Adversity 73

Drummer Louie Bellson was one of Duke Ellington's "steals" in the "Great James Robbery."

Heading Toward Newport

Duke Ellington's fortunes hit a nadir in 1954 and 1955. Though he had new band members, he did not yet have a new audience. Those who came out to hear the Duke play were mostly the same patrons who had come in the mid-1930s. One interview brought the question straight to the Duke:

> Q. Well, do you ever get tired or playing those old perennials night after night?
>
> A. No, this is a responsibility we owe people. Say, for instance, someone comes along who says, "We were married to 'Caravan,'" or "I met my girl at the Blue Note when you were playing 'Mood Indigo.'" It's important to them. We were playing one night some place down in Georgia when three people came up. "I met my wife," the man said, "for the first time when you were playing 'Sophisticated Lady,' and we danced together. It's a strange thing that you should be playing in our hometown on our daughter's twenty-first birthday!"[4]

Adversity 75

While he obviously relished the loyalty of these longtime listeners, the Duke realized that he needed fresh blood in the audience. The Newport Jazz Festival gave him the much-needed opportunity.

The Duke Ellington Orchestra's performance at the Newport Jazz Festival in 1956 electrified the young crowd.

The Revival

Duke Ellington and his musicians were invited to perform on the third and final evening of the 1956 Newport Jazz Festival. They arrived in good spirits, but the delivery of their "new" material fell flat. It wasn't until the Duke brought out "Diminuendo and Crescendo in Blue" that the audience responded.

Duke Ellington had composed this song eighteen years earlier, at a very different time in his life and career. It was unlikely that a song written in 1939 would appeal strongly to the very different crowd, composed primarily of young people, in 1956. But there was magic that evening, and Duke Ellington seized upon it. No one knows whether he intended tenor saxophonist Paul Gonsalves to play so many seemingly improvised repeats, but once the charm was released, it made excellent sense to keep it going.

By 2:00 a.m. on July 7, the Duke's career had been reborn. He successfully introduced himself and his orchestra to thousands of young people. If each of them told only three friends about this wonderful sound, that was enough to result in new, much-needed record sales.

Chapter 9

Return to the Top

The Newport Jazz Festival of 1956 brought renewed vigor to Duke Ellington and his orchestra. Though the best of his composing days were behind him, the Duke still had lots of energy to give his performances, and his tour schedule expanded, both in terms of dates and number of performances, in the decade that followed. There were bumps in the road, however. One of the most noticeable came in an *Ebony* magazine interview with his wife, Edna Thompson Ellington.

Private Matters Become Public

The Duke had long concealed the fact that he was still married to the woman he had gone to the altar with in 1918. Though they lived completely separate lives, the Duke and Edna remained legally married.

This fact did not prevent the Duke from having affairs. One hesitates to count, or name, the long list of women associated with Ellington over the decades. He moved from one woman to another, and, ever adroit at covering

78 DUKE ELLINGTON: Legendary Composer and Bandleader

Though they spent most of their adult lives apart, Duke Ellington remained legally married to Edna Thompson Ellington until her death in 1967.

his tracks, Ellington managed to keep his dalliances out of the press most of the time. He usually managed to deceive almost everyone, but the *Ebony* article exposed his neglect in the most painful way.

"We were going to Armstrong High School [back] then," Edna declared. "Duke wanted to be a commercial artist. I wanted to be a music teacher."[1] This was neither surprising nor controversial. But Edna went on to relate the difficulties of a musician's wife, especially one so committed to his art. There was no room for her, or for their son, Mercer, she asserted. The interviewer gently worked Edna around to the present day, essentially asking why she remained married. And there, in the pages of *Ebony*, was the answer: "You see I'm still hooked on Ellington."[2]

On learning of the interview, Duke Ellington was furious. He managed to cover his feelings in public, but privately he lashed out at everyone involved.

Returning to Europe

The Duke Ellington Orchestra made several trips to England and other parts of Europe. On one of these trips, Queen Elizabeth II asked how long it had been since the Duke's last visit. Perhaps his memory failed him, but the Duke replied that it had been in 1933, "before your Majesty was born."[3] The queen took no offense at the statement, and Ellington later composed an entire suite in her honor.

England and continental Europe were about a decade behind the United States, so far as popular music was concerned. Duke Ellington and his musicians, therefore, received stronger audience applause overseas than at home. The Duke knew, however, that the up-and-coming generation had different ideas where popular music was concerned. But for the Duke, if it sounded good, it was good music.

Honored at Home

By 1969, Duke Ellington seemed like a man whose time had come and gone. The shot in the arm provided by the Newport Jazz Festival was now thirteen years old. Critics continued to praise Ellington's classics, but they lambasted his most recent attempts. The death of Billy Strayhorn in 1967 meant that the orchestra was denied its second leading composer.

One of the biggest honors Duke Ellington ever received was the Presidential Medal of Freedom. In April 1969, the Duke and his sister, Ruth, went to the White House for an evening with President Richard M. Nixon and First Lady Patricia Nixon.

The president was an amateur piano player who had long delighted in the Duke Ellington sound. Nixon beamed as he quoted the Ellington song, "It don't mean a thing (if it ain't got that swing"). For his part, the Duke was charmed

Return to the Top 81

President Richard M. Nixon honored Duke Ellington with the Presidential Medal of Freedom in 1969.

Strays

Billy Strayhorn, nicknamed Strays, was, quite possibly the most underrated of the long-running Duke Ellington orchestra. Strayhorn enjoyed moments of real triumph, as when he composed "Take the A Train," but many listeners—jazz devotees among them—did not realize the extent of his contributions. But for Ellington, it was clear that Strays was invaluable: "Billy Strayhorn was my right arm, my left arm, all the eyes in the back of my head, my brain waves in his head, and his in mine."[4]

Duke Ellington heaped praise upon Billy Strayhorn in the weeks and months that followed his death, including making an entire memorial album, ...*And His Mother Called Him Bill* in Strayhorn's honor, featuring Strays's last composition, "Blood Count."

to be part of the White House scene. He got back to his hotel at 3:00 a.m., and ten hours later he was aboard a flight for the Midwest to play yet another series of dates.

A Spiritual Shift

Almost no one anticipated that Duke Ellington would make a move toward sacred music. He had been part of the secular music scene so long that he seemed like a fixture. But in the late 1960s, the Duke showed a renewed interest in spiritual matters.

Return to the Top   83

Ellington's religious practice was highly idiosyncratic. Some were surprised when he made a turn to religious music late in life.

On a private level, Duke Ellington had always been a deeply religious man. His practice was quite unconventional, but he was utterly serious about it. In the year that followed his beloved mother's death, he read and reread the Bible three times. Thereafter, he prayed every day, almost always in private. Only on rare occasions did he go to formal church services, but the depth of his religiosity was known to all his close associates.

While a departure from his previous work, the Duke's "sacred concerts," as they would come to be known, reflected all of his influences: jazz, blues, dance, gospel, and classical music. In 1966, Duke Ellington released *A Concert of Sacred Music*, a recording of his orchestra's live performances at Fifth Avenue Presbyterian Church in New York City. Though he would release two more albums of sacred performances, this first would be the most successful. His 1967 song "In the Beginning God," nabbed the Duke a Grammy and critical acclaim.

Chapter 10

Ellington in Perspective

Though he was still committed to making music, Duke Ellington slowed noticeably in 1973. His schedule remained full, but he limped through some of his concerts. No observable change was seen in his routine. Ellington continued to spend most of his time in hotels, eating the steak, grapefruit, and salad that had been his staples for almost forty years. But Ellington frequently seemed uneasy, as well as physically unsteady, onstage.

Some critics noticed the change. Others dismissed it, saying that the grand old man of 1930s music was still performing and had some years still remaining. But the worst was yet to come—and it came on quite rapidly.

The Last Concert

Even as he worked on his autobiography, which was scheduled for publication in 1974, the Duke gave one of his most ambitious concerts. The third and final of his

86 DUKE ELLINGTON: Legendary Composer and Bandleader

As the 1970s rolled in, Duke Ellington continued to perform.

"sacred concerts" was at London's famed Westminster Abbey in October 1973. The orchestra gave its all, but its quality had slipped noticeably. By this time, the music critics gathered that Ellington was in poor health, and they did not comment at length.

In the same month that he gave this last major concert, Duke Ellington suffered a severe personal loss. Arthur Logan, his personal physician and one of his best friends, died in New York City. Despondent, the Duke declared that it was over for him, that he would not last six months. His timing was close to spot-on. Duke Ellington died in New York City in May 1974, shortly after celebrating his seventy-fifth birthday.

The First Response

Thousands of people filed past Duke Ellington's casket. More than ten thousand people came to his funeral, held at the Cathedral of Saint John the Divine in New York City. The response was one of sadness and a sense of cultural finality: an era died with Duke Ellington.

He had been present almost at the birth of jazz, and he had played his way right through its highest moments. The Duke was the most prolific American composer of the twentieth century, and he may have played more concert dates than anyone else in the music business. Ellington was there for the Jazz Age and the Big Band era, and he still performed well, right into the 1960s, the decade when rock and roll took over as the premier form of popular music.

Could he have done any more for popular music? Very likely not. But he *could* have done more for his musicians.

The Talent of a Duke

Was Duke Ellington a musical genius? Or a very talented mimic? These two questions go to the heart of the Ellington story.

That the Duke possessed an amazing ear is undeniable. He could "hear" when a sound or song worked or did not, and he could make a decision with lightning speed. This helps account for his ability to lead the orchestra with a minimum of formal practice time. That the Duke could improvise was obvious. He could pick up a tune and move with it faster than any other big band musician. But this still leaves the all-important question: was the Duke an original composer?

That the Duke stole is undeniable. One of his earliest hits, "Creole Love Call," was practically lifted from the music of a rival musician. But Duke Ellington stole from his home base as well as outsiders. Time and again, he heard something

Ellington in Perspective

Ellington at a 1973 rehearsal for his final sacred concert at Westminster Abbey

90   DUKE ELLINGTON: Legendary Composer and Bandleader

Composing and playing until nearly the end of his life, Duke Ellington built an unforgettable legacy.

Ellington in Perspective

good performed by one of his musicians, reworked it, and made it his own. Was this theft? In the Duke's own time, it barely passed ethical standards. By our own twenty-first-century standards, it fails completely.

But while Duke Ellington's creative shortfalls are clear, one thing is equally clear: the Duke brought magic to the music. Audiences in the 1930s heard it, the audience at the 1956 Newport Jazz Festival rediscovered it, and—no matter how much musical tastes change—contemporary audiences will recognize it well into the future. The Duke was a magician who possessed genius, and who often got by with sleight of hand, but who always put on a good show.

Chronology

1899
Edward Kennedy Ellington is born in Washington, DC.

1914
Known as the "Duke" to classmates, he enters Armstrong Technical High School.
World War I breaks out in Europe.

1915
Ruth Ellington, the Duke's only sibling, is born in Washington.

1917
The United States enters World War I.

1918
Duke Ellington begins as a bandleader. His group is known as the Duke's Serenaders.

1919
The Duke marries Edna Thompson.

1920
Mercer Ellington is born.

1921
America officially enters the Jazz Age.

1923
The Duke and his musicians play in Manhattan for the first time.

1925
The Duke and his players are at the Kentucky Club.

1927
The Duke's orchestra begins a long engagement at the Cotton Club.

1929
The Great Depression begins with the stock market crash in October.

1931
"It Don't Mean a Thing (If It Ain't Got That Swing)" is recorded.

1933
The Duke and his orchestra tour England and France.

1935
Daisy Ellington, the Duke's mother, dies of cancer. Ellington writes "Reminiscing in Tempo."

1937
The Duke's father dies.

1939
The Duke and his orchestra tour Western Europe, just prior to the outbreak of war.

The Duke meets Billy Strayhorn.

1941
Ellington and his orchestra perform in *Jump for Joy*.
"Take the A train" is recorded.
America enters the Second World War on December 8.

1942
Ellington's orchestra suffers three serious personnel losses.

1943
Black, Brown, and Beige is performed at Carnegie Hall.

1956
Ellington's career is reignited at the Newport Jazz Festival.

1959
Edna Ellington is interviewed by *Ebony* magazine.

1966
The Duke performs the first of his sacred music concerts.

1969
Ellington receives the Presidential Medal of Freedom from President Nixon.

1973
The third and final sacred music concert is held in London.
Ellington's autobiography is published by Doubleday.

1974
Ellington dies in New York City.

Chapter Notes

Chapter 1
Rebirth at Fifty-Seven
1. "Jazzman Duke Ellington," *Time*, August 20, 1956, p. 55.
2. Ibid.
3. *Time*, p. 56.
4. *Time*, p. 58.

Chapter 2
A Capital Time
1. Edward Kennedy Ellington, *Music Is My Mistress* (Garden City, NY: Doubleday, 1973), p. x.
2. Ellington, p. 6.
3. Ellington, p. 15.
4. Ellington, p. 23.

Chapter 3
A Medley of Music
1. Geoffrey C. Ward and Ken Burns, *Jazz: A History of America's Music* (New York, NY: Alfred A. Knopf, 2000), p. 52.
2. A. H. Lawrence, *Duke Ellington and His World* (New York, NY: Routledge, 2001), p. 6.

Chapter 4
Leader of the Band
1. Mark Tucker (ed.) and Duke Ellington, *The Duke Ellington Reader* (New York, NY: Oxford University Press, 1993), p. 15.
2. Robert Gottlieb (ed.) and Duke Ellington, *Reading Jazz: A Gathering of Autobiography, Reportage, and Criticism from 1919 to Now* (New York, NY: Vintage Books, 1996,) p. 34.

Chapter 5
Sudden Fame
1. Terry Teachout, *Duke: A Life of Duke Ellington* (New York, NY: Gotham Books, 2013), p. 1.

Chapter 8
Adversity
1. Terry Teachout, *Duke: A Life of Duke Ellington* (New York, NY: Gotham Books, 2013), p. 10.
2. Edward Kennedy Ellington. *Music Is My Mistress* (Garden City, NY: Doubleday, 1973), p. 467.
3. Ellington, pp. 461–462.
4. Ibid.

Chapter 9
Return to the Top
1. Marc Crawford, "A Visit with Mrs. Duke Ellington: Musician's Wife Lives Quietly in Washington," *Ebony*, March 1959.
2. Ibid.
3. Edward Kennedy Ellington, *Music Is My Mistress* (Garden City, NY: Doubleday, 1973), p. 455.
4. Ellington, p. 156.

Glossary

adroit Extremely skilled or talented.

alto A voice or sound that is above the deep sound of a tenor, but below the higher tone of a soprano.

ascendancy A notable rise to power or fame.

compatriot A friend or peer.

divine providence The intervention of a holy power.

finality A sense of closure or ending.

gimmick A trick or manipulation used to sell or persuade.

Great Depression An era between 1929 and 1939 marked by a nationwide economic crisis.

hypochondria Irrational fear that one is ill or unwell.

mantra A personal creed that one repeats to oneself for strength and courage.

nadir The lowest possible point.

noncompliance Not following or going along with instructions or expectations.

urbane Suave, sophisticated.

Further Reading

BOOKS

Brower, Steven, and Mercedes Ellington. *Duke Ellington: An American Composer and Icon.* New York, NY: Rizzoli USA, 2016.

Cohen, Harvey G. *Duke Ellington's America.* Chicago, IL: University of Chicago Press, 2010.

Teachout, Terry. *Duke: A Life of Duke Ellington.* New York, NY: Gotham Books, 2013.

WEBSITES

Duke Ellington – It Don't Mean a Thing (1943)
https://www.youtube.com/watch?v=qDQpZT3GhDg
A video of a performance of "It Don't Mean a Thing (If It Ain't Got That Swing)" by Duke Ellington and his orchestra.

***Jazz Profiles* from NPR | Duke Ellington: The Pianist**
https://www.npr.org/programs/jazzprofiles/archive/ellington_pianist.html
An overview of Duke Ellington's talent as a pianist, with audio clips of musicians he worked with.

The Official Website of Jazz Legend Duke Ellington
http://www.dukeellington.com
The official website of Duke Ellington.

Index

A

Aldridge, Ira, 54
Anderson, Elaine, 13
Anderson, Ivie, 53–54, 62, 65, 66
Armstrong, Louis, 53, 54
Armstrong Technical High School, 29, 34, 79

B

Bellson, Louie, 72
Bennett, Tony, 49
Big Band era, 7, 47, 71, 87
Bigard, Barney, 66
Black, Brown, and Beige, 68–70
Blanton, Jimmy, 66
"Blood Count," 82
blues music, 43, 84
Brooks, Harvey, 29
Brown's Band from Dixieland, 25
Bud Shank Quartet, 11

C

"Camp Meeting Blues," 43
"Caravan," 74
Chaplin, Charlie, 65
classical music, 25, 84
Concert of Sacred Music, A, 84
Cotton Club, 39, 40–42, 43
Creole Jazz Band, 43
"Creole Love Call," 42, 43, 88

D

depressions, 45, 47, 48
"Diminuendo and Crescendo in Blue," 12, 76
Douglass, Frederick, 72
Duke's Serenaders, 31, 34
Duke Ellington Orchestra, debut of, 40, 42

E

Ebony magazine, 77, 79
Elizabeth II, 79
Ellington, Duke,
  autobiography, 20, 85
  comeback, 7–13, 74–76, 77, 92
  early life, 15–22, 28–30
  honors, 13–14, 72, 80, 82
  last concert, 85, 87
  personal life, 34–35, 37, 54, 56–57, 70–72, 77, 79, 85
  publicity stunts, 70–72
  revues, 62–63, 65–66
  spiritual life, 56, 82–84
  start as bandleader, 31–39
  sudden fame, 40–47
Ellington, James, 17–18, 20, 35, 56, 57, 71
Ellington, Mercer Kennedy, 34–35, 79
Ellington, Ruth, 35, 80

Europe, James Reese, 25, 26, 28
Europe, touring in, 47, 49, 53, 58–60, 79–80, 87

F

Frank Holliday's poolroom, 20

G

Garfield, John, 63
Gonsalves, Paul, 12, 76
Goodman, Benny, 7, 13, 49, 66
gospel music, 84
Grammy Awards, 84
Great Depression, 45, 47
"Great James Robbery," 72
Greer, Sonny, 31, 38–39

H

Hamilton, Chico, 11
Harlem Hellfighters, 26, 28
Harlem Renaissance, 40, 42
Hodges, Johnny, 66
Howard University, 38

I

"I Got It Bad (And That Ain't Good)," 65
"In the Beginning God," 84
Irvis, Charlie "Plug," 38
"It Don't Mean a Thing (If It Ain't Got That Swing)," 48–49, 56, 80

J

Jackson, Rudy, 43
James, Harry, 72
jazz, history of, 23–28, 34
Jazz Age, 23, 37, 87
Jazz on a Summer's Day, 11
Jeffries, Herb, 63, 65
John Wesley A.M.E. Zion, 20
Jump for Joy, 62–63, 65–66

K

Kennedy, Daisy, 17–19, 20, 35, 56, 57, 71, 83
Kennedy, James, 17

L

Lady Gaga, 49
Lincoln, Abraham, 15
Logan, Arthur, 71, 87

M

Miley, Bubber, 38
Mills, Irving, 45, 47, 58
"Mood Indigo," 74
musical revues, 62–63, 65–66
Music Is My Mistress, 20, 85

N

Nanton, Joe, 48
New Negro, The, 40
New York Fifteenth Regiment, 26

Index

Newport Jazz Festival, 8, 10–13, 74–76, 77, 92
Nixon, Patricia, 80
Nixon, Richard M., 80

O

O'Day, Anita, 11
Oliver, Joe "King," 43

P

Palladium, 53
Perry, Oliver "Doc," 33
Presidential Medal of Freedom, 80
Pullman porters, 22

R

ragtime, 23, 25
recessions, 48
"Reminiscing in Tempo," 56
Robeson, Paul, 42
rock and roll, 87

S

Sinatra, Frank, 8, 71
"Sophisticated Lady," 60, 74
S.S. *Olympic*, 49
"Star-Spangled Banner, The," 10
stock market crash, 45
Strayhorn, Billy, 60, 62, 63, 66, 82
Sugar Hill, 62

superstitions, 48, 71
Swing era, 48, 66

T

"Take the A Train," 12, 60, 62, 63, 82
Thompson, Edna, 34–35, 77, 79
Tizol, Juan, 72
Truman, Harry S., 72

W

Washington, Booker T., 72
Welles, Orson, 65
Westminster Abbey, 87
"What You Gonna Do When the Bed Breaks Down?," 34
Whetsol, Artie, 38
White House, 72, 82
Wilhelm II, 26
Wilson, Woodrow, 26
World War I, 25–28, 30, 35, 58
World War II, 7, 58, 59, 62, 63, 71

Charlotte Etinde-Crompton

Samuel Willard Crompton

About the Authors

Charlotte Etinde-Crompton was born and raised in Zaire and came to Massachusetts at the age of twenty. Her artistic sensibility stems from her early exposure to the many talented artists of her family and tribe, which included master wood-carvers. Her interest in African American art has been an abiding passion since her arrival in the United States.

Samuel Willard Crompton is a tenth-generation New Englander who now lives in metropolitan Atlanta. For twenty-eight years, he was a professor of history at Holyoke Community College. His early interest in the arts comes from his wood-carver father and his oil-painter mother. Crompton is the author and editor of many books, including a number of nonfiction young adult titles with Enslow Publishing. This is his first collaboration with his wife.